No Surrender
A Field Manual for
Creating Work With Heart

+NO+SURRENDER+

A Field Manual for Creating Work With Heart

by

Paul Waggener

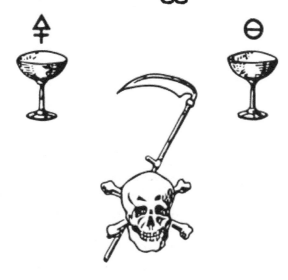

PWLiberI

CONTENTS

FOREWORD by ANGEL SUAREZ

"*My whole life I watched everyone else play by the rules that they had been told were sacred- in mundane life and spiritual practice— and go deep into debt on college educations that placed them in some shitty job they never wanted in the first place, or break their bodies on the rack of thankless manual labor. I saw armchair magicians paying dues to have worthless titles conferred on them by old men more interested in kinky sex than spiritual transcendence. So I kept playing by my own.*"

The first time I met Paul was the summer of 2016.

The night we met, I watched him walking—it was one of the few times I saw someone who moved with utmost and violent purpose.

And the world moved with his intent.

Since then, the mystery of the man has not diminished—and he certainly has not slowed down.

On the contrary, to know Paul is to only find yourself more and more amazed by his ability to transform and drive himself at virtually any cost, with no signs of slowing down, no worries about discomfort or difficulty.

The other night, for example, we were sitting in his living room. It was far too late, close to 5 AM at least while we passed a bottle of Knob Creek Bourbon back and forth.

Paul was telling me about his success over the last few years—financially, physically, with his tribe, his wife.

But these were brief, fleeting subjects next to the beast which dominated our dialog: how he could go even further.

How he could *stop being comfortable*, ending the stagnation of complacency.

How he could *stop* taking it easy.

What he could do to train harder, get stronger, be even more successful.

Taking it further, why he would even want to do these things.

Why would he want to go further than anyone could reasonably ask?

Most people race towards STOP signs.

They're seeking an end; they want the catharsis of a conclusion, or the illusion of 'done.'

The reality of the human condition is not to seek ceilings, but to find just enough standing room to indulge the fantasy that you've escaped a cage.

The book you're reading, right now, is the answer to that question in many ways.

Paul is one of the few people I've met who doesn't languish in his successes. He's the first person to look in the mirror and say, "What have you done for me lately?"

Quoting the man himself,

> "To cultivate endurance means simply, becoming hard as fuck. We can never allow ourselves to entertain thoughts of failure, or "rest stops." There is no secret behind this."

Knowing Paul, reading his work, and seeing the nuances of his decisions day by day with his personal life, his business, his friendships, you see that he is someone who connects the 'web' of events at every moment.

One thing you do does not exist in a world unto itself. It is not an isolated creature running amok with no repercussions.

By viewing every action, every decision, as a brush stroke on the greater canvas which is the portrait of your life, you begin to grasp the weight of your actions.

Things take on more gravity, and the idea of resting on your laurels, watching your name, body, and legacy wilt away becomes more unacceptable.

This book, *No Surrender*, is the weapon to rage against such a doom.

It is Paul's furious onslaught—a fist crushing the notions of mediocrity and "settling."

In it, he says,

> *"We are thoughts in the mind of god—each of us an idea taking form over the course of our lives, as the massive cosmic organism flows and changes, with us, a tiny neuron or flickering insight that it has during its unimaginable life-span."*

There is an inferno of Holiness, and each man can be a torch burning in the dark with it.

Or he can be the smoldering ruin, left behind on the black road, forgotten.

This book is flint and steel.

It is a lighter.

It is a match.

I've been endlessly inspired by Paul—as a thinker, as a fighter, as a friend, and as a brother.

He is someone who won't let himself "take it easy," and won't give his friends the siren luxury of it either.

Let this book be that for you.

Let it drive you to seize the only form of immortality any man or woman can hope for.

And to quote Paul:

"Create accordingly."

INTRODUCTION by PAUL WAGGENER

I got started on this road early in life, while I watched everyone else play by the rules that they had been told were sacred, and deeply questioned the value of those rules. From my childhood years spending a lot of time in church, to later in my teens seeing friends go deep into debt on college educations that ultimately placed them in some shit job they never wanted in the first place, or while at various times I broke my body alongside them on the rack of thankless manual labor- I did my best to discover and play by my own rules. I was homeschooled for most of my childhood but never "finished" high school, and I never went to college, although I was offered a music scholarship, but turned it down to move back out West and work as a roofer in my teens.

I spent those teenage years working alongside convicts and meth addicts, lifting some weights and first discovering a love for that, but no real discipline for it yet.

The rest of life before twenty could be summed up by a lot of extremely hard partying, writing, drawing and playing in punk and heavy metal bands.

A lot of the usual teenage stuff: getting into a lot of fights and sleeping with women (sometimes the latter fed into the former), traveling around the country by greyhound bus, that kind of thing.

The not-as-usual: practicing magic and doing every drug I could get my hands on (although historically the two go hand in hand, I have found that my esoteric practice has helped me break habits and addiction more than it panders to them), selling drugs (this as a short lived business endeavor utilized at different points in my younger years only when money was needed as an emergency—I never liked the risk/reward ratio of selling illegal materials), starting a back alley fight club that made it onto the FBI's desk and resulted in my first few real run-ins with law enforcement, and starving in shitty hotels.

My twenties were focused more heavily on music, but addiction and poor choices were still very prevalent.

There are years of that decade I can't remember, or can only bring back in little pieces, as alcohol use continued and opiates became an everyday indulgence. I'd kick bad habits for a little while and get back into weights and other fitness endeavors, but always fell off my discipline and wound up back in the hole.

I played a ton of shows, toured a little; discovered a love of making money unconventionally by promoting and hosting shows at an old farmhouse outside of town; got fully addicted to opiates, wrote a lot, drank a lot more; fell in love a few times, got my heart broken a few times; kicked the drugs and got kicked out of the show house; went back to work in construction, got married, watched it fall apart, the whole while getting cleaner and leaner and starting to see a glimmering light of purpose somewhere in the distance. At one point in my mid-twenties, I moved to a little cabin in the woods with no power or water and stayed out there for a year to see if I could do it. I spent a lot of time fasting, testing my physical limits with sweat lodges and cold river water, went a little crazy and fell in love with the silence and the coyote's singing and named the pair of horned owls that lived out there with me.

It was during this time that I really began to develop the world-view and mythopoetic mindset that is so important to me now, and I look at it as one of the most formative times of my life. It was a withdrawal from everything that was so desperately needed at this stage- a detoxification on many levels. I had quit smoking cigarettes, and drinking was lessened to a major degree as I had begun kickboxing and doing jiu jitsu with friends in an abandoned building we shared with a herd of goats. Lots of fond memories of the "Goat Gym" and the guys who trained there.

After that idyllic period, I moved back into the city and kept writing, kept working out, kept drawing and deepening my understanding of myth, magic, willpower and who I was, where I fit in to all of it.

Through this entire time, my goal was always experience.

More experience.

Trying to fit more than a lifetime's worth of action and activity into a single year than most people got to live in a decade.

My first marriage went south, which doesn't need to be hashed out here, but suffice to say it was a real kick in the head. I remember tearing off into the night and fog on my motorcycle in a pair of old camo shorts, no shoes, no helmet, no shirt—wide open throttle and just losing my mind.

I went a little crazy for a year, at the time making my entire living on playing music. I just fell back into old habits—hit the bottle like it owed me money and started using pills again, until a year of that put me in the hospital with a heart attack. I think I was 29 that year, and having a heart attack was a pretty crazy experience, but I didn't slow down just yet.

Somewhere in that endless cycle of rot and redemption, I started a concept called Operation Werewolf.

It began as an idea that was me, in the way that I most wanted to be—a perfect ideal that I could live up to if I gave it everything I had, and sacrificed everything I was for everything I knew I could be.

The project began as a simple workout journal, which I still have, complete with pep-talks to myself to stay off the smokes, keep away from alcohol and so on. A tightly scribbled, non-stop inner monologue from my higher self to my lower, offering tough love, encouragement, and, where necessary, brutal criticism.

Every day I did my best to bring myself in line with that voice a little more.

I understood what it was telling me a little more deeply. In so doing, I found that I was changing my own life and inspiring myself to greater action, and it stuck.

I finally got serious about weight training, and started doing some martial arts again. Addiction was put solidly in check and held there. While on tour and figuring it all out, I met a woman and eventually married her, and for the first time experienced a relationship where my partner reinforced rather than ripped apart all the things I was trying to develop, which was a new experience for someone who had been exclusively in toxic relationships in the past.

During the next few years, until the present time, Operation Werewolf grew as a concept and began bringing people together around the world, who were ready for life reform and the pressure of a community of people trying to make each other better. It has been my honor to meet and call many of those people friends.

Sometimes, the simple problem in this life is that we forget to ask ourselves the questions:

What do I want to be?

What do I want to do?

What is it that will fill me with fire?

What could I wake up doing each day that would make me truly satisfied with the road I was on? We have to know ourselves, so we have to ask these questions in order to determine our own purpose. Without a purpose, everyone is just flailing around like a bad swimmer who's gone out too far into the deep water, looking for someone to save them from their own poor planning. In this world, there's no lifeguard coming to save you.

Your entire existence can boil down to walking through life with no idea of where you want to go or who you want to be, and then you just sort of... die.

My purpose, in its simple form, is to make myself someone I would want to be friends with. To always be looking to make myself better, and in so doing, inspire other people to be better. Stronger, smarter, wealthier, whatever it is they want to be.

I've always been able to get people excited about doing whatever it was I wanted to do, which is ultimately a pretty selfish and unsatisfying thing.

Now, I do my best to get people excited about what they want to do.

Through this project, and all the connections I've made from it, I've gotten letters and emails from people telling me I've helped un-fuck their current life situation, deal with depression, overcome stress and anxiety, get fit, kick drugs, forget heartbreak, make more money, and a hundred other things, all with the same technique:

> I just do my best to help them find a purpose, to create work with heart, and, in the meantime, to become healthier and stronger—since I don't believe an unhealthy body leads to an environment in

which we are likely to be able to fulfill that purpose once we find it.

Once they have that, and they understand dedication and discipline and can begin to master them, it's off to the races.

This book is not for everyone, which is a good thing.

Everything is not for everyone.

If you want to get to the next level, and the next one and so on, and you recognize that Nietzsche was right when he said that the only good thing in this world is the feeling that one is overcoming, that power is growing, then maybe this will jive with you.

Maybe it won't. Take it or leave it. For those who recognize its value and are able to put its concepts to work for them: I'll see you out there.

Personal freedom comes at a heavy price, and some of what follows might seem extreme. In my experience, only the extreme will ever find success and lasting independence in this world, because there is no place at the table for the mediocre except beneath it, begging for scraps.

Keep rising.

—PW

NO SURRENDER:

*A Field Manual For Creating
Work With Heart*

I.

Everyone wants more money.

Sure, there may be a few monks on a mountain somewhere who have transcended the desire for the finer things in life, but for the rest of us, money means access, power and leverage.

Eating good quality food, exploring the world, the security of our own home, reliable conveyance, medical treatment when necessary without going into crushing debt, even supporting those within our network through patronage by buying or investing in their endeavors- none of this can be done without wealth.

In the pre-Christian era of Europe, wealth was seen as a noble pursuit, one that led to respect, power, and leverage.

In Hinduism, they called this pursuit "artha" and it was seen as one of the ways to live a meaningful life, when approached in a virtuous fashion.

A chieftain in pagan Europe was largely successful or unsuccessful due to charisma and open-handedness, that is, his ability to attain enough wealth that he could be generous with it, thereby establishing loyalty and love from his inner circle and soldiers, in order to attain even more of it.

Likewise, the great holy festivals and rites of pagan worship throughout the world were largely dedicated to success of some kind— whether battle or trade, prosperous fields and livestock or conquest in other lands to expand the means and territory of the tribe or people.

The Celts and Germans were known to throw gold and silver into sacred lakes in order to receive a like gift in return from their gods, ancestors or the genius loci, showing an undeniable connection between wealth and their religious practices.

They did this because they understood a simple truth.

Money is power.

People don't really want money simply to buy nice things, although that is one undeniable and pleasant side effect of having money. But at its core, everyone knows that money represents power in this world, and everyone wants to be more powerful.

This is what we have to change our minds about, and our attitudes. We have to stop looking at wealth as a strict currency, some dirty money that exchanges hands in strip clubs and back alleys, or exists as one's and zero's in our bank account, some finite, small concept.

Instead, we must understand the mystery of currency as a power source that fires the circuitry of possibility. That's what money is. A tool to leverage possibility.

I heard it said somewhere that increased responsibility meant greater power, but that when we are dependent on someone else, we are relinquishing power. This single idea pretty much sums up my entire attitude and philosophy toward money.

I don't want to relinquish power over myself to anyone else.

I want to hold the reins, and I don't want to spend my life crushed and beaten down by debt, poverty, reduced opportunity, tightly scheduled labor for pay, or seeking the generosity or openhandedness of greater men.

Better men.

Because in this world, no one is equal.

No one is equal in any way—unless they are.

If I can lift 500 pounds off the ground and you can't, I am stronger than you at the deadlift. No if's, no and's, no but's.

If I can't multiply 12x12 in my head and someone else can, they are smarter, more learned than I am.

If you can't afford to fix your broken down truck and I can, it makes me more powerful than you, on a temporal level.

These ideas affect everything—how strong we are, how tough, how wealthy, how good-looking, or charismatic. The people that say they don't matter are the ones who don't have any of that shit, and can only fling slander and jealous barbs at those who do.

The fact is, it all matters. It all dictates our place in the world, our social standing in the world, and in our own in-groups. We've evolved to admire those who are capable of thriving, capable and skilled at acquiring.

Whether that is acquiring strength or wealth, or "getting girls," or anything else, we respect those who can ably "do for themselves." We look down on those who are always looking for hand outs, the self-willed weak, or the socially inept. This comparison, these judgements, they happen all the time, every second, every moment.

The reason that wealth and power is the most important of these, is that in this world, it dictates more areas of your life than anything else.

To have or to have not.

To go do what you always dreamed of, or to be stuck at home in some shitty apartment watching other people doing what you wanted to do and saying "one day, one day."

One day is right.

One day you'll either understand that in order to live lives of legendary excellence, of liberated action, we can't be dependent on anyone but ourselves- or one day, you'll die unfulfilled.

The choice is completely up to you how you want to go out, but I can tell you this from personal experience: if you are someone who has big goals, massive dreams, wild, expansive thoughts, creativity, charisma, or whatever else- none of it matters if you're stuck in the meat grinder of wage slavery.

The pursuit of wealth and power is the game of kings.

It is the high stakes dice roll that harshly marks the line between rulers and ruled, slaves or free men, and make no mistake that this is the true nature of the world whether you like it or not. The concepts and realties of power, wealth and rulership do not require our approval to simple "be."

Wealth is a storm. A lightning bolt that we can harness to power the entire machinery of our complex goals, plans and network, and allows us to create an empire in the desert.

We can either hold the reins or stay under the whip.

In order be free, you have to be a rebel. Like Lucifer in Christian mythology, you have to first be willing to cast of the shackles of someone else's rulership and be willing to "reign in hell, rather than serve in heaven."

It is the ultimate trap to be lulled into complacency by an easy paycheck that doesn't require much more of you than that you show up and do what you're told. My father used to call this "the golden handcuffs," a job that you despise, but are bound to because you can't walk way from the money.

You must be a rebel, because in order to become something of your own creation, someone reliant on himself, dependent on himself, and only answering to himself, you have to break down the fear of this rebellion—you must commit to a war against being ruled over by others, and seek your own kingdom, even if it kills you. Anyone who decides to not pursue this kind of life is ultimately either a coward, or has already surrendered the reins to someone greater and admitted defeat before he has ever struck the first blow.

No matter how much he makes, he will always depend on the boss, and never be the boss himself.

You must be a rebel because anyone who wants to make money for himself must commit utterly to this lifestyle. He must burn his ships, and do away with any notion of a safety net. A safety net or an escape plan only exists for those who intend to fail, or who are riddled with the fear of failure too much to ever succeed.

You will only fail if you let your attention and focus waver—you must pursue your goal at all times, and let it consume you. Anything less will lead only to downfall, and ruin.

II.

The only thing that will lead to success in self-employment is integrity and genuine content, which I call "Work with Heart."

Whether you are an artist or musician, a copywriter or clothing designer, those of us who are filled with the entrepreneurial spirit to live lives on our own terms have one thing in common: we are creators.

As a creator, you are either one with Heart, or one without heart. There is either a fire burning inside, or your work is empty and hollow, a clay model without a soul, a bad Xerox, lifeless and grainy.

The first thing to understand is that your life and your brand are not distinct from one another: they are One. There is no line between what you are, what you do, what you create. People say all the time that you have to "separate the art from the artist," which I have always thought was bullshit. The art IS the artist, and vice versa, otherwise his work was without heart, and was just an artifice, or a lie.

Because of this, the most important thing to cultivate is experience, and from experience, authority. In whatever your given field is, you have to deserve to exist there by putting in years of work toward becoming a living representative of whatever that field is. An archetype.

You can't set out to create a successful brand by avoiding paying your dues, and this is one of the ways heartless work can easily be identified: has the person trying to hawk his services paid those dues? Or is he a 19 year old touting himself as a personal trainer? A twenty something selling himself as a life coach? These people will always play themselves, and walk right off the edge of the cliff built by their own hubris.

They cannot create work with heart because they have not cultivated experience, and distilled that —gathered in a specific niche.

Don't make the mistake of placing the cart before the horse. Find your purpose, and then live it with every second. The Work cannot be something to dread, or avoid, and if it is, quit now, and spare yourself the embarrassing and inevitable failure of those who produce heartless work and are found out as the frauds they are. Always put in the time honestly, with everything you have.

Work with heart must be work done with the entire heart.

That work is the mission and you must be the killer that undertakes it, ruthlessly, brutally and without mercy for yourself—you wanted this, you got it. Every detail, every moment, every waking hour, that's what it will require of you.

If that fills you with dread or trepidation, you're in the wrong racket. Go get a fucking job at the mall. If it fills you with excitement, and your mind starts to run over with ideas, plans, calculating angles and the strategies of warfare, you may have what it takes to be your own man. In the motorcycle world, chopper guys will often say "chop what ya got," by which they mean, whatever motorcycle you already have is the one that you should work on building, instead of worrying about "the perfect one" to work with. This holds true here, as well.

The question I've gotten the most from guys wondering what they should be doing is "Where do I start?" The answer, of course, is, wherever you are now.

Unfortunately, there's a certain amount of incorrect spirit in the question itself—"what should I do?" "Where should I start?" These kind of questions imply an aimlessness or confusion or heartlessness that simply will not do in this world.

I can't answer the question of what you should do, only you can do that.

But here's a headstart, and you may have heard it before from others:

> What would you do if money wasn't a factor at all?

The answer to the question is more than likely your salvation, and you've been sitting here overthinking it this whole time, believing that is was more complex than that, or that whatever that answer was wasn't good enough.

It doesn't really matter if the answer is "sit around and play video games" or "write a screenplay" or "lift weights and jerk off," or whatever it is—there is a market for it out there. If you are so passionate about writing a screenplay that every morning you wake up completely on fire to do it, that it dominates your thought processes and screams through your neurological pathways like a freight train— it's what you should be doing.

How you will live off that is another matter, but if you apply yourself with full heart, you could write a blog about screenwriting, sell screenplays, sell coaching (if you're worth a damn), hold seminars and mastermind groups for screenwriters, start a private paid forum where famous screenwriters come on and answer questions- you name it, the sky's the limit.

(If you like to lift weights and touch yourself, there's probably already a website that offers lifting videos, coaching, tutorials, nutrition planning, and pornography all in one place. If it doesn't—knock yourself out.)

Once you have decided what you will do, what your purpose is, your Holy Mission, you have to treat it as such. You have to give it the care and respect it deserves. Feed it with fire and blood, and it will feed you back.

When I make a post, write an article, create a product, or make a video, I follow these rules:

First, I pretend that I am paying to make the post or write the article. In some cases, as in boosting or advertising content, it is quite literal, but I carry this mentality into every use of my website or social media. If it cost you 100 dollars to make the post, or release the article, video, whatever, would you still do it?

Is it so aflame with your message and in line with the spirit of your brand that you would drop a C-note just to get it out there? If your answer is no, then go back to the drawing board and put your whole goddamn heart into it, and then press that "send" button like you are launching a nuclear weapon at the whole world, with nothing but zeal and conviction in your heart.

Second, I imagine that it will be the only thing anyone ever sees, hears, or reads from me. Ever.

This is an extreme tactic, but it is really helpful for me. Is this one article such a solid representation of the spirit of my brand that if it was the only thing I ever released, I could live with that? Would I be okay with this being what was read at my funeral, something that totally matched up with the definition of who and what I was trying to become?

Remember, we ARE our brand, and if that doesn't hold true, you are creating heartless work.

If your work is with heart, there is no dividing line between you and the brand. It is your job every single day to make that statement more authentic and true, until you are a living, glowing sigil that reflects the pure light at the center of your mission.

Third, I pretend that a million dollars is at stake. If the writing or speaking or artwork is not good enough to catch the eye of the discerning, someone who totally resonates with my brand but wants to see something so distilled, so pure, so aflame, that it changes their life, and they give me a million dollars for it—it isn't good enough.

These kind of mental exercises before you post on social media or release an article will keep your eyes on the prize, ensure that you are working with your whole heart, and not wasting your or anyone else's time with sub-par garbage.

If you are a creator, you are in the business of changing lives. If you're not changing lives with your work, your work is heartless. Take responsibility for that, and act accordingly. Hold yourself to a higher standard than anyone else could possibly ever hold you to, and be irreproachable.

This will automatically eliminate things like wasting time on social media, one of the great killers of those who work with the internet. If your time is precious, you won't waste it. If your time isn't precious, or worth everything to you, then your work is heartless.

Those who work with heart know that every minute counts, because they are trying to light the world on fire with the creations. With every moment spent on their brand, they act as though they are planning a murder or starting a new religion, and they take the weight seriously.

They are not creating cheap plastic garbage, useless trinkets, clickbait trash or fake news. They are putting their heart on their sleeve, without complaining, without lying, without laziness or carelessness, because it is everything to them.

They don't pretend to be something they're not, they just put their head down and keep on becoming it, more in line with who they want to be every day, because they know that their own life is an ongoing act of creation, and that this life is their brand—they look to become living symbols.

Because of the serious and extreme nature of our work, it must also be done free of distraction. We owe it to ourselves, and to those who believe in our work to eliminate the noise and chatter from our lives while we create, otherwise our work will be all static and noise and chatter.

When you sit down to create, destroy illusion and distraction by removing it from your workspace. Your workspace is your temple, and everything in it must be holy and in consonance with your work—you are the High Priest here, and everything in your surroundings must influence and increase the integrity and strength of your Holy Mission.

Inspiration should come from within and without, so adorn that temple of creation with things that inspire you and fill you with fire. These things can take many forms, but start with a clean slate each time you sit down to work.

Maintain an orderly temple, and keep it clean, and organized.

Listen to music without lyrics, to keep your thoughts focused and free of outside influence from other creators—that is for times of experience and distillation, not for times of creation. When we create, we need to be alone with our thoughts and ideas, and although they are often amalgamations of many other things, when we create, we want to be free from obvious influences like these.

Hang artwork that creates resonance. Listen to music that keeps focus and calms.

Turn off the internet and phone. Be a vessel for your higher self, and always remember to keep your full heart fully involved.

If you use someone else's work, always give credit where it's due—no one likes a thief.

Go outside often throughout the day, and allow it to cleanse you and purify your intention, and shake off the madness, only to give yourself to it again when it is time. Make no mistake, these acts of creation are a divine mania that descends on us like possession, and if you create without this ecstatic connection, it is because your heart is not full.

Wake up early and get started. Don't oversleep. Everyone says you need 8 hours of sleep, but I've never found this to be true, and do just fine in a very active life with quite a bit less. The feeling one gains from having accomplished several things for the day's list by 8 am is one of power and focus, and it breeds more of itself.

Keep a notebook to schedule your day. The importance of this cannot be overstated.

Don't neglect your exercise. Creatives understand that keeping the body healthy and active keeps the mind healthy and active, so practice martial arts and lifting and/or running. The body is a chariot for the god that lives in your mind and in your heart, and to let it fall into disuse and ruin is a cardinal sin for the creator.

Don't neglect your mind. Meditate and breathe at some point throughout the day to defragment and attain some silence. This is very important for those of us possessed with the divine madness of creation—it will drive us crazy if we cannot put a stop to it. I recommend several minutes given over to meditation and breathing at the beginning of the day, and again at the end of the "work day," to free up space, after you have written down everything you need to do the next day and all your plans and battle strategies.

This way you can let go, settle down, and enjoy your life, knowing you are prepared for the next day, the next engagement, the next battle. You can be at peace, and not feel like you are forgetting something or missing something.

This mission is intact, and you are prepared to again Work With Heart.

III.

I have, over the last few years, watched organizations and brands rise and fall like the winter wheat. Those who fancied themselves creators throw themselves with reckless abandon into building up a brand, blog, tribal outfit or business, only to be nowhere to be seen within a few months or year.

Almost everyone who starts doing this will quit for a few reasons, or fail for the same ones.

These pitfalls, however, once identified, can be avoided by the daring and intrepid.

The first, and possibly the simplest, is a lack of focus. Unable to remove distraction from their path, they cannot seem to get out of their own way. Always on their phones, or out partying, or moving around too much to find the quiet calm at the center of the storm—this is the place where the creative must live.

Like Odin in Norse myth, those seeking to create Work With Heart must exist in the eye of the hurricane, using the chaos of the winds and flying debris as their own building blocks to success. They must be able to find strength and clarity in the middle of the madness, and not only this, they must be able to thrive there.

Life is chaotic. Life as a creative, and one who works only for themselves, can often seem like an electrical storm of responsibility, details to remember, calendar dates, lists of "to do's," and a thousand minutiae flying this way and that, too many things to ever perform at once, and the weak are overwhelmed and beaten down by it.

Instead of calmly grasping one straw out of the air at a time, and then another, and another, they see only a blinding mass of unachievable details, blurring together and defeating them.

We must achieve focus. We must eliminate distraction.

Robert Greene, author the excellent books *Mastery*, and *The 48 Laws of Power*, states:

"In the future, the great division will be between those who have trained themselves to

handle these complexities and those who are overwhelmed by them—those who can acquire skills and discipline their minds and those who are irrevocably distracted by all the media around them and can never focus enough to learn."

To destroy this limitation and overcome it, there are basic strategies.

The first is to begin meditating, and gain control over the swirling inner universe. The complexities of meditation presented by the modern guru are often overwhelming by themselves, and I think it is largely over complicated by those looking to sell you something.

Start by taking ten minutes in the morning, sitting down comfortably, and focusing only on your breathing. Don't worry about "thinking about nothing," it is much easier to have a point of focus.

Every time your thoughts wander, bring them back to your breath. Focus on inhaling slowly through your nose, holding the breath for a moment, and exhaling a slowly as you can, using your diaphragm the entire time. Don't get too caught up in "right and wrong."

Even just doing this one simple exercise will give you more control over your mind and the chaotic spiral of your thoughts and desires. It isn't some hokey new-age bullshit—think of it as reps in the weight room. If you do something correctly enough times, a positive result will occur. There is a plethora of information out there on the positive effects of meditation that you can lookup for yourself.

The next strategy for focus is keeping a journal. I've outlined some of this already in previous sections, but I can't overstress the importance of this. Clearing out your mind and making lists of things you need to accomplish in order of importance gives you a razor sharp understanding of what needs to be done that day.

It will give you a leg up on anyone not doing it. Use pen and paper, not digital. The mind connects more strongly with handwritten notes than it does typing or texting.

I also favor a "scorched earth" policy when it comes to achieving focus for work. Remove anyone and anything that detracts from your focus, or remove yourself to somewhere else.

I have a very difficult time writing or drawing with others in the room, even if they are being unobtrusive—it drives me crazy. Ditto for songwriting, and any other creative work. The simple solution to this is to either let the people in your life know that you will be working at a set time, and that you need to not be distracted (i.e., they need to leave), or you need to find a Haven.

A haven is a place you can go where there will be absolutely no distraction. Coffee shops, lobbies and so on are a terrible choice, since there are always people in and out. A library is a better choice if you can find a secluded back area, since almost no one seems to go to them these days.

Even better is an office. If you are deep in the throes of the creative process and are struggling to focus, or the people around you or who live with you are blocking that process, go get an AirBnB or a hotel. Nothing can come between you and the creative process—be as extreme as necessary. Go to fucking Antarctica if you have to.

For me, 4 hours of completely undistracted work is usually enough to accomplish a huge amount of fiery labor—compared to hours of dealing with intrusions and so on, during which time my focus can waver and my attention wander.

Turn off your phone completely when creating. Disconnect the wi-fi on your laptop. The notifications and other garbage that will pop up during your work will pull your brain elsewhere, and you can't afford this. Your work demands a pure and smokeless fire.

Some people like speed, or pills to achieve a point of focus, but I have eschewed these methods in favor of noise canceling headphones with lyric-free music or binaural beats, isolation, and a lot of coffee.

I don't recommend that people take drugs, but if you are truly a creative, you will use whatever it takes to give birth to the work which will transform the world. You will do anything, overcome anything, destroy anything, and eliminate anything from your life that gets in the way of this process—because you must complete the process.

If it isn't absolutely necessary to your creation, get rid of it.

The phrase "hell is other people" is very accurate when talking about the process of creation. Not due to any fault of theirs, but your own.

It is always when you are attempting to focus like a blade on your immediate goals that you will be invited to the best parties, road trips, bars, or even simple outings.

As a creator, you must learn to say "no" ruthlessly and often. Entertainment and "fun" is a luxury for after you have accomplished your task- it cannot be engaged in during the war of creation. If it is your priority, you will never accomplish the Work With Heart. Have fun later—it will still be waiting for you.

The second reason for failure and surrender is a lack of conviction.

Belief in oneself should never be confused with cockiness, hubris, or overconfidence—these are the traits of the insecure.

Conviction, however—an utterly unshakable faith in one's mission, and the truth and righteousness of their goals and creations—this is absolutely necessary for the creator. It cannot be missing from his heart, or his work will be timid, uncertain, wavering, and deserving of annihilation in the fires of truth.

Examine yourself.

Is your work True? Is it eternal? Are you creating it for all time? Is it making the world more interesting, fearsome, inspired, ugly, or fascinating?

Is it CHANGING THE WORLD?

You must believe in what you are doing with the faith of a suicide bomber. If your zeal is weak, you are weak, and your work is weak. It must live inside you like a bonfire, and when people look in your eyes, they have to see the flames of your holy mission burning there, an obsession that should border on the insane.

If it falls short of this, it is not enough.

Conviction, also, must stand up to the test. Anyone who performs Work With Heart will meet with that friend called Resistance. Resistance itself is a powerful ally and teacher, although it will often manifest itself through enemies, hollow men and the envious or jealous. Sometimes it will manifest through the creator himself as he deals with burnout, distraction and so on.

Any belief that will not stand and grow stronger in the face of resistance is not a conviction. It is a hobby. A little pink bubble waiting to pop at the slightest pressure.

You must feed your convictions through self-examination, and through examining your work, maintaining a high level of focus, maintaining the fire that burns within, shutting down external criticism- unless founded. Never underestimate the value of well-founded criticism, but learn the difference between useful critique and jealous shrieking.

Most of the time, looking to the outside is a mistake made that shows a lack of conviction. It is not always wrong to seek advice and the words of wisdom that can come from confidants and close friends, but this is your journey, not theirs. It is your mission—they are on their own, and so even if they are well-meaning, they will give words filtered through the fire of their own crusade, and its value can be limited by this.

Look to your own heart for the words and advice you need. Seek the higher self always- it is the divine in you that will come to your aid and see you through the hard times. It is the north star in the darkness that you can always count on, even when all other things seem false. Believe in it utterly.

Thirdly—failure comes from a lack of consonance.

I have written about consonance a great deal, as I believe it is the highest key to discovering satisfaction and power in this life. Consonance is, as Nietzsche said, the organization of the chaos of one's passions.

At first, life seems like a series of events and concepts and a thousand lights of illusion pulling in all directions. Many will never see its underlying patterns and lines, and they will exist in a constant state of chaos, of wandering, and of confusion. They will never attain consonance.

If you have ever done hallucinogens, you will perhaps understand what I mean- when you looked at trees or buildings deep in the grip of lysergic acid or psilocybin and became suddenly aware of the way all of it made perfect geometric sense.

Every branch and leaf falling perfectly at divine angles, a sacred geometry of every seemingly disconnected thing fitting together just so.

In our lives, this must be artificed. The canvas of our lives and passions must be given scope from above, from within and without—it must be chaos given order by our own hand, until all of our interests, passions, pursuits, actions and words all twist together like a DNA helix, spiraling and wrapping around one another in a symmetrical form, moving together to create a totally consonant whole.

Since brand and creator are one, this holds true in the world of business, art, branding, everything. Everywhere.

Your message must be clear and undiluted. Every image, every word must support another, creating a framework that even the uninitiated can see clearly with the naked eye. All feeding back into the center, from furthest branch to deepest root, like a tree. All fed from the same fire within your heart, all fashioned to the same greater purpose, and visible form and function.

Lack of consonance is dissonance. Dissonance is tension, clash, chaos- and it is death to both brand and creator.

Every time you create Work With Heart, it must be tested and checked, like a hammer tapping against metal—every note must be in harmony with the rest of your brand and creation. This does not mean everything must be the same and create a boring note of monotone — a monotone cannot have consonance, because there is no interplay to create the consonance. Your work must instead be like notes on a musical scale, or within a chord, creating depth and texture in your work, but a depth and texture that is pleasing and flows.

Ask yourself: is this image perfectly in line with the mission? Are these words, this art, this song, this logo, whatever it is, is it creating flow or blockage? Is it harmonious with everything else in my brand, or does it not "fit?"

Change can occur within a brand, but it must be gradual, like a composition—people do not like dissonance. Human beings desire consonance even if they are unaware, and when they see it in a brand, they recognize it unconsciously, just as they will recognize and be repelled by dissonance.

Always maintain it in your work.

The fourth and final reason for capitulation is the lack of endurance. Although none of these four are more important, and all are totally required, endurance is the one that many who have the others in spades will find themselves lacking.

Endurance is the hardest to achieve because it takes the rest of our lives, and as such is the longest challenge we will ever undergo.

There are so many snares, challenges, ordeals and traps along the way, that most are simply unable to maintain forward momentum for very long. Their spiritual fire is extinguished quickly and easily by life itself, and they swiftly return to their comfort zone, and often will never recover.

Quitting is habitual, just like success.

If we cultivate the act of endurance, it will grow, and our fire will increase, our "gas tank" will deepen, and we will be more capable of continuing through the next set of hills turns.

To do otherwise is to set into motion a continual and ever expanding web of failure and surrender that will grow into every area of our lives and choke every endeavor, every relationship, every act we will ever undertake with the chronic suffocation of "quit."

In order to endure, we must understand that the principle of perpetual motion is our greatest ally. To stop moving forward, even for a short period of time, is to allow our momentum to slow and stop. When rolling a heavy stone, it is much more taxing to get it moving again than it is to simply keep it moving, without fail, world without end, amen.

To cultivate endurance means simply, becoming hard as fuck. We can never allow ourselves to entertain thoughts of failure, or "rest stops." There is no secret behind this.

It is mental and spiritual toughness gained through encountering soul and mind crushing fatigue or difficulty, and gritting the teeth until blood runs from the mouth, moving forward in the face of boots kicking and opponents punching, not giving in, struggling to breathe, feeling like you are drowning, one foot in front of the other, can't stop, will not stop, strike back, power forward, rend soft meat from the bone, smell blood in the water, attack, attack, attack.

It cannot be learned. It can only be attained by doing.

Endurance is a critical and crucial key to attaining entrance through the gates of the true creator. The one who will be at this endeavor forever, until death steals the final breath from his lungs, and he can die with a grim satisfaction that his work will live on forever.

Read Homer's Iliad. Read the Bhagavad Gita. Read the Rig Veda, or the Kalevala. Consider how long they have existed and survived. Consider the mental state of their creator. Consider that these works have traveled through time to reach you, to affect you, to do the intended work on your internal universe and alter your reality.

Create accordingly.

IV.

In the 1976 film "Network," one of the characters states:

"I don't have to tell you things are bad. Everybody knows things are bad. It's a depression. Everybody's out of work or scared of losing their job. The dollar buys a nickel's worth, banks are going bust, shopkeepers keep a gun under the counter.

Punks are running wild in the street and there's nobody anywhere who seems to know what to do, and there's no end to it. We know the air is unfit to breathe and our food is unfit to eat, and we sit watching our TV's while some local newscaster tells us that today we had fifteen homicides and sixty-three violent crimes, as if that's the way it's supposed to be.

We know things are bad—worse than bad. They're crazy. It's like everything everywhere is going crazy, so we don't go out anymore. We sit in the house, and slowly the world we are living in is getting smaller, and all we say is,

'Please, at least leave us alone in our living rooms.

Let me have my toaster and my TV and my steel-belted radials and I won't say anything. Just leave us alone.'

Well, I'm not gonna leave you alone. I want you to get mad! I don't want you to protest. I don't want you to riot—I don't want you to write to your congressman because I wouldn't know what to tell you to write. I don't know what to do about the depression and the inflation and the Russians and the crime in the street.

All I know is that first you've got to get mad. You've got to say, 'I'm a HUMAN BEING, God damn it! My life has VALUE!'"

We live in interesting times. I say interesting, not "bad," because for me, there is no "good" or "bad," and strange times and interesting ones beat boring ones. In fact, I believe the time I live in is the exact moment I need to exist in, as though it was tailor made for me to do my Work.

We live in a time like no other—and those of us who are Creators are alive at a time where we can thrive and operate like never before. This time has given us so many tools with which to work, to create our own reality, to be our own kings and queens, that anyone who complains about it is a loser. A wimp. A punk.

Times for us are not bad—they are interesting. They present that exciting word—opportunity. For me, that opportunity is adventure, and that is exactly how I see my brand.

I am able to center my entire life, not around hour after hour spent in a damn cubicle somewhere, ticking the minutes off my bland existence for a chance to "have a cold one with the boys" at some barbecue in a manicured backyard identical to every other one on the block- but to really LIVE.

I can train hard and spit blood, ride motorcycles around the country, lift weights, brawl in back alleys, hike in the mountains, take strange plants and meet the gods who live in them, sleep in tents or under the starry sky—and I can do all of this while running my business/brand, because this IS my business and brand.

It is critical that we maintain this spirit of adventure in our brand, in our lives, in our very bones!

That we don't give up or give in, ever, for any reason, and we continue to see life for what it is: a wide open world meant for us to experience, create within, explore, and learn from, but also to enjoy, to be beaten down by, to grasp and distill as much as possible before the fire dies in our hearts forever.

We are thoughts in the mind of god—each of us an idea taking form over the course of our lives, as the massive cosmic organism flows and changes, with us, a tiny neuron or flickering insight that it has during its unimaginable life-span. I would like to be a good idea—an idea that takes root and expands into an undertaking, an undertaking that spreads into myth, a myth that endures in the very mind of the cosmos.

Whether or not any of this is objectively real or true is of absolutely no consequence for me- I choose to live as though it is.

And because of this—I cultivate obsession, and a conqueror mindset.

My allegiances are only to my brand, and to those individuals in this world who resonate with it, and I with them in turn. I never create for anyone else, and this is another powerfully important idea:

YOU ARE ONLY EVER CREATING WORK FOR YOURSELF AND THOSE WHO UNDERSTAND AND FIND RESONANCE WITH IT.

Never, ever, under any circumstance, compromise your vision or ideals in order to make them more palatable or easy to digest for anyone, for any reason. Work With Heart is challenging, and made to challenge.

Work that is without heart is bland, easy for the masses to grasp and digest quickly, like plain white rice or tofu. In a world of tofu, be a bloody steak.

As you strive to make each day an adventure, to crack the longbones of life and suck out the marrow, more and more accurately representing the very core of your edicts, ideologies and philosophies with every action, remember that for you, there are no excuses.

The magician, the creator, he never says things aloud like "I am not good at that," "I can't," or "I don't have time." He learns, and becomes better—he gathers up the intelligence and knowledge that exists everywhere in the world around him and becomes capable of many things, in order to be more self sufficient. If he lacks the aptitude, he does not lament it—he weighs the value of investing the time to learn it, or he hires someone who is already excellent and pays them their dues.

He has no patience or mercy for "I can't" and sees only challenges, puzzles, games, and opponents to best.

He knows that every single person has the same amount of moments in the day, and he spends them wisely, like an investor, in the things that matter to him. He never lies and says he doesn't have time. He understands that every minute, every second is a choice, and a sacrifice of every single other thing he could have done- but didn't. He lives with his choices, and constantly weighs and examines his expenditure of that most valuable resource at his command.

He eliminates fear and is always seen at the front of the battle, where the fires burn hottest. The creator knows that the best generals lead from the front, dauntless, inspiring courage and conviction in those around them, and that as a creator, he will build up an army around himself. Whether these are supporters, allies, followers, clients, or otherwise, he must view them as the troops available to him in the war as he builds an empire, a kingdom, a city state.

He lets his armies see that he is the highest representation of what he has stated as his Holy Mission, and he leads the crusade, holding the banner high, and walking through the fires that alight around him, tongues of fire like lotus flowers in his footsteps.

As you march, know that the stones and arrows that fly like a hailstorm to slow or stop your progress can only find weak spots in your armor if you let them. These stones and arrows are unfounded criticism, the jealousy and envy of hollow, weak people, too concerned with tearing others down to build anything of their own. These half-men will hate you the most, as they witness you at the head of your legions, annihilating where they are too afraid to go, conquering where they have surrendered, receiving the praise that they desire for themselves like a merchant covets gold. The helm you wear is called obsession, and the armor you wear is called indifference.

Through the slit in your visor, you can only see where you are going, the Grail, as its illumination drowns out these vampires and shadow creatures. Keep your eyes fixed on the wholesome, the uplifting, the mission, the war. Let them dissipate like smoke in the light of your victories.

Speak little of your goals to others. Keep your plans within the confines of your mind and heart, and let their fire and pressure build, driving you onward to completion. Too much talk will lessen their power and explosive force, and will cause you to lose interest, having already spoken of it, and released some of its power into the world, it can no longer detonate.

Your future goals should be guarded and protected like battle plans from the enemy. Let your actions simply unfold to the rest of the world, and "let success be your proof." In this fashion, your enemies and competitors can only witness where you have been, while being completely in the dark about where you will strike next, or where your forces will appear.

Don't overthink- trust your intuition. As you develop your mission, it will grow within you, and all things will filter through it. You have to have faith in it, and yourself, always. Motion is often better than meditation, and paralysis can result from analysis, as they say. Action, sometimes any action, is the key to shattering the stasis that can and will occur on your road to success.

Believing you are capable of anything will make you capable of anything- not right away, perhaps, but in time. Just because god provides for the birds doesn't mean he puts the food directly into their nest. If you are passionate, and dedicated, you will find a way to attain the things that you need, by hook or crook.

Always remember that there is more than one road to attainment of nearly everything, but one constant: it must be earned, by blood and fire.

V.

Moving forward with your mission can be easy at first, when there is so much fresh experience, so many things to build, to create from scratch, like the Garden of Eden, where everything has just arisen from the primordial waters and you are a young god in your new kingdom.

Years past this beautiful and incredibly rewarding phase, you may find yourself considering a Great Flood to utterly destroy and erase everything you have created as you watch it spiral into places you never wanted or expected. It might feel bloated, a great hulking thing with malignant growths and a thousand loose ends spinning off of its bulk as it crawls, slug-like, and directionless across the landscape.

You may be burned out, exhausted to a level far beyond where a simple edict to "endure" can reach you, as you struggle with things like existential crises, self-doubt, or cataclysmic life events.

I call this the "68 Comeback Special."

Elvis had been spending a lot of time out of the public eye, forgoing live performance and music for movies, running his empire, and watching his image change into something different than where he had probably intended at the beginning of his career.

Long story short, in 1968, the King came back with a bang—lean and mean, in black leather and the curling lip sneer that was so iconic—he came out onstage and just killed. It was everything Elvis represented: mean, surly, nasty, but so ultimately likable, capable and dominating of a presence that no one could help but say: Elvis is still the King.

If you've gotten anywhere near this point, it means that you've done what few others could do in the first place, by taking an idea to a point where you can even experience something like true burnout and exhaustion, but you can't fall prey to it.

It's time for your "68 Comeback Special."

First, find a way to cessate all work and creative activity for a period of time between 1 and 3 months. As a creator, this will be a special kind of agony, but you need the time to recharge your batteries—don't fall for the premature recharge at a week or two in. If you start up again too soon, the burnout will return, and worse than before.

Travel during this time. Go to a white sand beach or ride motorcycles in the Himalayas. For more practical approaches, check out for a bit, and just avoid the same old hangouts.

Embody the Hermit card, or spend time with friends—whichever is more uncommon for you.

This time is about allowing your natural energy stores to recover, to completely come back from the chronic low they have been at, for the reactor to "cool" if you will, in order to handle the heat and energy that is about to come.

Maintain this distance for as long as is necessary—you may have to plan for this well in advance in order to keep your finances in order and so on, but it's the only way, so however you need to make it happen, make it happen.

This is Superman returning to the Fortress of Solitude. It's Jesus wandering in the wilderness. It's Siddhartha setting out on his journey in order to attain enlightenment.

Treat this spirit journey with the attention and seriousness it deserves, because what comes next is going to require every single bit of focus and force you've accumulated over the last years of being a creator. Burnout is a test, and one of the most dangerous and potentially enervating things that a creative can experience—don't underestimate its ability to destroy everything you've worked so hard for, and set your empire in ruins.

Somewhere in this time period, you will feel the stirrings of your old self. You will feel the coals begin to smolder again, and you will remember what got you into all this in the first place. There may be a definitive moment, or it might come as a slow burn that builds until inferno. However it happens for you, just let it happen. This is perhaps one of the only times in life where I recommend a more passive approach, because this mistress cannot be forced.

It is the spirit that is indwelling in your creative center, the goddess that resides unseen at the heart of the labyrinth that makes up your abilities, your mission, your everything. Allow her to reveal herself to you in her own time, and know that this is one of the most important periods of your life- recapturing your very Essence.

As the flame builds to white heat, you will use it to immolate—but you will do so selectively. Not with flood, but with fire, you will rebuild your kingdom.

Focus on the bloated parts, the unwanted parts, the malignancy that has attached itself to your creation, and blast them unmercifully with atomic spiritual fire. Rid yourself of all those aspects of your brand that are unnecessary. This is about burning things down to the framework, the powerful bones upon which your empire was built in the first place.

Your watchwords here are Lean and Mean. Everything that is fat gets the torch.

Remember the absolute attitude you had when you began, and find it again.

Start to work up a new strategy. Start a new notebook just for it, and program out this necromantic ritual of resurrection by staring at that blank white paper and knowing that the future is unwritten and your will is the ink that will begin this new era.

What do I want to be?

What do I want to do?

What is it that will fill me with fire?

What could I wake up doing each day that would make me truly satisfied with the road I was on? These are the only questions that matter. Pen the strategy. Write the future. Eliminate the unnecessary, the unwanted. You are absolute ruler of your own destiny, and it is your edict that will determine your path, and no one else.

Take control again. Be fucking Elvis, and make your comeback better than anything you've ever done.

Remind the world why you are who you are, and why only you can do what you do.

The freedom that this world, this way, this life provides, is there for the taking, and if you won't reach out and take it, you don't deserve it.

No retreat.

No remorse.

No surrender.

Until next time—I'm pulling for you.

—PW

"Waggener isn't playing at life, he's living it, and he's writing to inspire others to do the same — to go out and become the kind of men they dreamed about being when they were younger, while they are still breathing."

Jack Donovan.

www.paul-waggener.com

Made in United States
Orlando, FL
30 November 2021